HOLY WORD OF JAPUJI SAHIB JI
(As I Understood It)

HOLY WORD OF JAPUJI SAHIB JI
(As I Understood It)

Meditate The Most Beautiful And Powerful

AMRIK SINGH BINAPAL

Copyright © 2020 by Amrik Singh Binapal.

ISBN: Softcover   978-1-9845-8393-2
          ebook   978-1-9845-8392-5

All rights reserved. No part of this book may be reproduced or transmitted in any form or by any means, electronic or mechanical, including photocopying, recording, or by any information storage and retrieval system, without permission in writing from the copyright owner.

Any people depicted in stock imagery provided by Getty Images are models, and such images are being used for illustrative purposes only.
Certain stock imagery © Getty Images.

Print information available on the last page.

Rev. date: 06/17/2020

To order additional copies of this book, contact:
Xlibris
1-888-795-4274
www.Xlibris.com
Orders@Xlibris.com
815561

CONTENTS

PART 1 INTRODUCTION TO THE SUBJECT

Introduction to the Subject..1
'Japu' as a means of Meditation 2
The art of Give and Take 3
Acknowledgements..4

PART 2 ATTRIBUTES OF GOD

!! Ik-Onkar !!..7
!! Sat-Nam !!..9
!! Karta-Purkh !!...10
!! Nir-Bhau !!..11
!! Nir-Vair !!...12
!! Akal Murt !!..13
!! Ajuni Sebhn !! 14
!! Gur Parshad !! 15
!! jap !!..16

PART 3 THIRTY-EIGHT STEPS TO REACH HIM

!! Step First !!..21
!! Step Second !!..25
!! Step Third !!...27
!! Step Fourth !!...31
!! Step Fifth !!..34
!! Step Sixth !!...38
!! Step Seventh !!...41
!! Step Eighth !!...43
!! Step Ninth !!..45
!! Step Tenth !!..47
!! Step Eleventh !!...50
!! Step Twelfth !!..52
!! Step Thirteenth !!...54
!! Step Fourteenth !!..56
!! Step Fifteenth !!..59
!! Step Sixteenth !!..61
!! Step Seventeenth !!..66
!! Step Eighteenth!!...69
!! Step Nineteenth !!..72
!! Step Twentieth !!..76
!! Step Twenty First !!...79
!! Step Twenty Second !!...83
!! Step Twenty Third !!...85
!! Step Twenty Fourth !!..87

!! Step Twenty Fifth !!...91
!! Step Twenty Sixth !!...95
!! Step Twenty Seventh !!...100
!! Step Twenty Eighth !!...104
!! Step Twenty Ninth !!..106
!! Step Thirtieth !!...108
!! Step Thirty First !!..110
!! Step Thirty Second !!...112
!! Step Thirty Third !!..114
!! Step Thirty Fourth !!..117
!! Step Thirty Fifth !!...119
!! Step Thirty Six !!..121
!! Step Thirty Seventh !!..123
!! Step Thirty Eight Eight !!..126
!! Closing Slok of Japuji Sahib Ji !!...128

PART 4 GENERAL

Realms of Achieving Him 133
About the Author 137
About the Book 139

PART ONE

Introduction to the Subject

Introduction to the Subject

It is universally believed that 'Japuji Sahib ji'
is the essence, the key to 'Holiest of Holy Word' of
"Sri Guru Granth Sahib Ji"

It is also believed that if any common or even an uneducated Man
is able to understand and apply the Spirit of this key,
he will surely be able to achieve permanent peace.

*Opening up the third eye, sixth sense and tenth door
after the realization of Eternal Truth,
any Believer will realize the fact
that "The One" whom we worship, pray and sing to
is in-fact nothing else other than His own Real-Self,
is nothing else other than his own Self Confidence.*

*It finally is our own state of
"Sat-chit Anand" "Puran Parm Anand"
"The Union of a Lover and Beloved"
which makes us sing and dance in the
State of Ecstasy.*

'Japu' as a means of Meditation

*"Stone, a rough and tough rock, we all know,
needs to be hammered again and again
to finally chisel out a beautiful Budha,
from its own within"*

*Staying focused on the Most Beautiful and Powerful,
Keeping our eyes always fixed on Beauty of Nature
which exalts our spirits is what exactly
the word "Japu" really means.*

*The routine and regular practice
of this Mantra of Holy word 'Japu'
is the way to 'Everlasting Bliss and Eternal Life' we seek.*

The art of Give and Take

When we are at peace, we can handle any situation
in a much better and productive way.

But when we are sad, upset or angry
because of any reason, we get confused.
Every small thing in that blush of anger or ego
gets more complicated and cumbersome.

When we Love everyone Un-conditionally,
pleasures of the world start flowing towards us.
And it happens by itself.

*Everyone born is blessed with some unique quality
of his own which identifies him.*

*Everyone has something in spare and reserve
to share comfortably with others but the tragedy
is that we, the non-believers, cannot even comprehend
the value hidden in the art of making use of this attribute
of respectful 'Give and Take'.*

Acknowledgements

The write up on this subject is accomplished
with Blessings of God at the request of
Dr. Navdeep Kaur Chhina, my daughter.

Dr Jagdeep Singh, my son helped me
In translating it from Punjabi to English.

Dr Nancy Singh Johal, my daughter-in-law
added to its beauty, using her computer skills.

Doing all this my attention was naturally focused
on the future of my grandchildren
Navi, Anmol, Avi and Eva
to see them finally emerge as decent
human beings and citizen of this world
and as accomplished professionals.

Everything of this project of course became possible
only with the silent support of the Captain of the Ship,
Mr Sukhjivanpal Singh Chhina, my son in law.

I thank and pray for the best of all my well-wishers.

PART TWO
Attributes of God

!! Ik-Onkar !!

(Significance of Spirit of Oneness)

He only is the One.
Immortal and Everlasting.
The entire "Cosmic Energy" of Universe.

The "Soul of Universe"
Stays always the same
In its Quantity and quality
Content and essence.

Never increases.
Never decreases.
Never decays and dies.

Melody of this Mysterious
'Ik-Onkar 'Dhunii'
when listened meditatively
establishes us in everlasting Bliss,
the perfect state of Equipoise.

In just a blink of an eye and in just one shot,
the 'Light' instantly appeared from this energy

became visible in innumerous kinds of colors,
shapes and sizes of His Creation.

Like the colors of a rainbow
which originate from One
colorless source Light,
this cosmic energy too has only one
'Zero-Sum Color'
'Unity in Diversity Color.

"Ik Onkar" is the 'Creator, Care-Taker and Replenisher
All the three in One
for His House of Beauty.

Like a good house holder,
He keeps his house always clean,
Regularly throws all old and used garbage out
and replenishes it with new to keep His house
Lovely, Lively and Fresh.

All this is the manifestation of One
which only is True.
Everything else is illusion, fog and smog,
the mirage of something
which just appears but does not exist.

!! Sat-Nam !!

(Significance of Word Sat-Nam)

His name is Truth, the word Sat-Nam

Whatever is happening in universe is not done
It happens by itself without any effort.

Whatever is happening by itself is 'Divine',
The Truth, the Will and Work of God.

Anything which is never prefixed,
happens by itself and stays forever
is the Spirit of Love
is the Spirit of Truth
is the 'Mark and the 'Name'
of the most Beautiful.

!! Karta-Purkh !!

(Creator-The Super Soul)

'Karta Purkh' is the Creator
The Guru and the Govind
Three in one.

With highest State of Awareness.
He is the Eternal Source of Light
And the way to Truth and Life.

!! Nir-Bhau !!

(Perfectly Pure and Fearless)

He only is perfect, Pure and Clean
Both inside and out.

He only is the one who is Fearless
And stays in His own kind of
Blissful State of Mind.

!! Nir-Vair !!

(Embodiment of Kindness and Forgiveness)

Hatred and Enmity to none.
He is an embodiment of
Kindness and Forgiveness,
Caring and Sharing
With whole of His Creation.

Doing so He stays always smiling
Always in high spirits.

!! Akal Murt !!

(Ever Existing Beauty of Nature)

Death-less and Evergreen,
He stays unaffected with 'Time and Space'
He stays unattached from negativities of
this illusionary and transitionary world.

He is the epitome of 'Beauty and Strength'
An embodiment of 'Inner Peace and Bliss'

!! Ajuni Sebhn !!

(Never Changing Essence and Self-Born Reality)

The only One
Self-Born Reality,
Never changing in its
Quantitative and qualitative Essence.

Totally free and independent from
the cycle of birth and death.
Maintains always the same
'Serenity and Equipoise'

Like water, the source of energy,
it maintains same attributes of
its 'Beauty and strength'
and all other Divine Qualities
even after passing through different forms
like that of vapors, clouds, snow and rain etc.

!! Gur Parshad !!

(Achieved with Blessings of the Gracious Guru)

With Blessings of
Gracious Guru, the Teacher
Gobind, the Creator
and His visible form of Creation,
we get freedom of thought and action,
The Peace and State of Immortality.

!! jap !!

(Chant and Meditate in Every Breath)

!! Aad Sach Jugaad Sach !!
!! Hai Bhee Sach Nanak Hosee Bhee Sach !!

He was true before He fixed His creation.
He is true now and will be true for all the
Times to come.

Yes, He only is worthy of
remembering again and again
through every breath of life.

Note:

The stanza 'The Shabad' expressed above
witnesses Unequivocally the existence of
creative being personified through words
instantly came from the mouth of Nanak
after his Smadhi in Vein River.

After this Shabad of Meditation,
the next Thirty-Eight steps have tried to explain
the un-explainable beauty and strength
of the fountain head source of Grace
thus trying to uplift the seeker to
His level of beauty and strength.

PART THREE

Thirty-Eight Steps to reach Him

!! Step First !!

(Significance of His Command and Will)

"Whatever happens at a specific time,
at a specific place is the sum total
of the set of circumstances
till that time"

This act of Nature
is what we remember as "Will of God"

Nobody has seen God but Yes,
He can be realized
'Through His Nature'
'Through His Creation'.

Nature is His Will, His Work,
His Grace and His Command.

Understanding and becoming one with Nature
is the way to Truth and Life.

Following His Will, Jesus Himself climbed the
hill with cross on his shoulders and prayed
for forgiveness to even those
who put Him on the Cross.

Sri Guru Arjun Dev Ji
sat in the State of Equipoise
on the hot iron sheet
meditating on the Holi Word
and prayed for the good of everyone.

!! Sochai Soch Na Hova-ee Jay Soche La<u>kh</u> Vaar !!
By thinking alone, no one can
assess and evaluate His Greatness,
understand and achieve Him,
thinking even hundreds of thousand times.

Absolute and Perfect cleanliness of
anything cannot be achieved and
maintained even by cleaning
hundreds of thousand times.

Absolute and Perfect in only the One
And that One is Him only.

With the constant burden of
superfluous thoughts at mind,
we get sick first at our mind
and then at the body.

!! Chupai Chup Na Hova-ee Jay Laae Rahaa Liv Taar !!
By keeping silence,
strictly mum all the time,
our mind does not stop
wandering and wavering.

Even in our dreams
we run from pillar to post
like a bubble of mercury
in a flat-base bowl.

This non-stop wandering of mind
due to misconceptions of
all prevailing Truth,
is nothing but an anxiety,
the beginning of all health problems.

!! Bhukhia Bhukh Na Utree Jay Bannaa Puree-aa Bhaar !!
The urge of 'Hungry' is not appeased,
even by piling up loads of worldly goods.

Sikander, the winner of world
finally died helplessly.

When someone dies under constant pressure
and unbearable stress of self-created mess,
he takes this garbage with him to the next world.

There too his mind revolves around 'Maya'.
the mirage of illusions.

Without diving deep into the perfect state of
satisfaction and contentment
and stabilizing our mind,
no one can exist peacefully.

!! Sahas Si-aanpaa Lakh Hohi Ta Ik Na Chalai Naal !!
Hundreds of thousands of worldly wisdoms
and clever tricks one may play,
not one of them will go along with in the end,
like that of Ravanan and Duryodhnan.

A crow who considers himself most clever and wise
finally dies at the stinking garbage.

Without blessings of
the most Graceful and His Creation,

without an honest and hard work living
without sharing something with 'Have Nots,
one cannot understand and appreciate
the real worth of his being in society.

The 'King of Kings', Dharm-Raj
will never accept and approve
mischievous acts from anyone
and in any circumstance.

!! Kiv Sachi-aaraa Hoeea Kiv Koorhai Tutai Paal !!
So how can we become truthful?
And how can the veil of illusion be torn away?

How can our house get enlightened,
in the shining light of which
we should gracefully be able to
embrace our Beloved achieving Peace
and Tranquility of mind?

!! Hukam Rajaa-ee Chal<u>n</u>aa Nanak Li<u>kh</u>i-aa Naal !!
No one has seen God but yes,
He works through His nature says Nanak.
The 'Laws of Nature' is His Command
which if followed up Truthfully
will surely Lead us to the destination
we finally wish to achieve.

'His Command' explained above
is not written anywhere in books.

It is already there in the psyche of
everyone's sub-conscious mind
like sweetness of the milk
and flavor of a flower.

!! Step Second !!

(His Command and Liberation from ego)

Ego shuts the doors of all human faculties
and the way to Truth and Life.

Humbling down deep to the Earth opens us
the doors to the 'Kingdom of God'.

Following His Command,
Bhaii Lehnan ji was honored
with kingship of both the worlds by Nanak.

Disobeying command,
Bhaii Sri Chand and Ram Rai
lost the Kingships from their own fathers
and wandered aimlessly in the world.

!! Hukmee Hovan Aakaar Hukam Na Kahi-aa Jaa-ee !!
His Command cannot be described in words
but by His Command,
bodies of innumerable sizes,
shapes and colors are created.

!! Hukmee Hovan Jee-a Hukam Milai Vadi-aa-ee !!.
By His Command only,

souls come into being
And by His Command only,
'Glory and Greatness' is achieved.

!! Hukmee Utam Neech Hukam Likh Dukh Sukh Paa-ee-ah !!
By His Command only some are high
and some others are low.
By His Command imprinted in our psyche,
pleasure and pain, heaven and hell are obtained.

!! Iknaa Hukmee Bakhsees Ik hukmee Sadaa Bhavaa-ee-ah !!
Some, by His Command are blessed.
And they achieve 'Salvation'
from the cycle of birth and Death.
Others by His Command wander aimlessly
in fog and smog of illusions.

!! Hukmai Andar Sabh Ko Baahar Hukam Na Ko-ay !!
Everyone is subject to His Command.
No one is beyond His Command,
The Sun, the Moon, the Stars and the 'Super Stars',
everyone follows His Command and works to His will.

!! Naanak Hukmai Jay Bujhai Ta Ha-umai Kahai na Ko-ay !!
One who understands His Command,
never speaks in ego and High-Headedness
of his useless and flimsy thoughts,
Says Nanak,
Humbleness down to the Earth becomes
the hallmark of his life.
It makes his vision clear to look
even beyond the galaxies.

!! Step Third !!

(Creator and His Ever-Blissful Nature)

He is in us and we are in Him exactly the way
a fish is in water and water in fish.

Appearing in many forms and colors
is the presentation of His Aromatic Quality
One Zero-Sum, Invisible Light appearing in
countless colors of His creation.

Most Cool, Calm and blissful by His Nature,
He is Independent of the effects
of Time and Space.

Like a lotus flower of the pond,
while keeping His roots firmly fixed in the pond,
He stays unaffected from the stink of pond.
He keeps Himself always in high spirits.

!! Gaavai Ko Taa<u>n</u> Hovai Kisai Taan !!
Those with power sing of His Power
because their mind is always attached
to the power of body mussel.

Sleeping, awaking and working,
they think and dream of the mussel
and the body built up.
They can never even think and envision
anything differently.

Their minds all the time wander
in wrestlers play-grounds just watching
as to how someone beats someone at one time
and then gets beaten by the same person
at the other time in the next inning.
This only becomes the sole purpose of their life.

!! Gavai Ko Daat Jaanai Neesaan !!
Some sing of His Gifts
like that of the good parents
A good wife and healthy children.

Some sing of their material wealth
and so many other things of luxuries
to make their life more comfortable and at ease.

This is the mark, symbol and sign
to prove their strengths
and acts of graciousness.

People remember Him for all such gifts.
and worship Him day and night.

!! Gaavai Ko Gun Vadi-aa-ee-aa Chaar !!
Some sing of His Glorious Virtues,
Greatness and Beauty
and aspire to achieve
same heights of glory one day.

!! Gaavai Ko Vidi-aa Vikham Veechaar !!
Some sing of the knowledge obtained of Him,
through difficult studies and exchange of ideas
Sitting around the table.

!! Gaavai Ko Saaj Karay Tan Khayh !!
Some sing that He fashions the body,
and then again reduces it to dust
like a skillful potter
who creates innumerable pots
of different sizes and shapes
to prove his art.

!! Gaavai Ko Jee-a lai Fir Dayh !!
Some sing that He takes away life,
and then restores it back
in different forms
at different times.

!! Gaavai Ko Jaapai Disai Door !!
Some sing that He seems very far away
at the highest peak of snow mountains
and even beyond the endless skies.

!! Gaavai Ko Vaykhai Haadraa Hadoor !!
Some sing that He watches over us face to face,
ever-present, close to the next breath
and next push of blood by the heart
to all parts of the body.

!! Kathnaa Kathee Na Aavai Tot !!
There is no shortage of those who teach,
preach continuously and consistently
about the way He works.

!! Kath Kath Kathee Kotee Kot Kot !!
Millions upon millions offer millions of
sermons and stories since the time eternal
to explain and express Him
the way He appears to them.

!! Day̲daa Day Lai̲day Thak Paahi !!
The Great Giver keeps on giving like the Sun
the gifts of life like heat, warmth and light
continuously, consistently and unconditionally.

While those who receive
sometimes grow very weary of receiving
and become astatics because of their inability
to bear the responsibility of sustaining heavy loads
for longer periods of time.

!! Jug̲aa Jugan̲tar K̲haahee K̲haahi !!
Consumers consume throughout the ages,
and sing His praises uttering 'Tera Tera',
that everything belongs Him and only Him.

!! Hukmee Hukam Chalaa-ay Raahu !!
The Commander by His Command,
leads us to walk on the path of virtues
and righteousness.
As is His will He commands.

!! Naanak Vigsai Vayparvaahu !!
Says Nanak,
He blossoms forth,
carefree and untroubled.
never tires, never breaks
and feels handicap in anyway.

!! Step Fourth !!

(Ambrosial Time, the best Offer to Please Him)

The best offering to Please Him
is the offering of Ambrosial Time
when both the Lover and Beloved,
when both husband and his wife
are sitting alone for prayers
in quiet state of their minds!

!! Saachaa Saahib Saach Naa-ay Bhaakhi-aa Bhaa-o Apaar !!

True is the Master,
True is His Name,
True is his justice.
Sweet is the language of His love,
the unconditional, ever existing
and infinite love.
Says Nanak,
Like Columbus
Trusting in Him only
he boarded the ship
with a hope that He, our Savior
will definitely streer it safe
to the destination we seek.

!! Aakhahi Mangahi Dayhi Dayhi Daat Karay Daataar !!.
People beg and pray, some by singing, some by dancing
and some others with a bowl in their hands uttering
"Give us, Give us"

And the Gracious Giver goes on blessing His Gifts
Unconditionally and un-interruptedly.

!! Fayr Ke Agai Rakhee-ai Jit Disai Darbaar !!
The question of all the questions therefore is,
that in the spirit of thankfulness,
what offering can we place before Him which
can make Him always maintain and sustain
the same level of kindness and compassion for us?

!! Muhou Ke Bolan Bolee-ai Jit Sun Dharay Pi-aar !!
What words can we then speak,
what services can we render
and what deeds can we perform to
evoke the same Love?

!! Amrit Vela sach Nau Vdiai Vichar !!
Offer of 'Amrit-Vela' the ambrosial hours before dawn,
when our conscious and sub-conscious mind
are half awake and half asleep
and when they silently interact and talk
to each other to resolve mutual conflicts
and serious problems sometimes
disturbing our sleep and peace,
is the most appropriate gift to offer.

Focusing, meditating and chanting
True Name at that time
and contemplating His Glorious Greatness,
is the best and the right way to go

and the right offering to appease
and please Him.

‼ Karmee Aavai Kaprhaa Nadree Mokh Du-aar ‼
By the karma of past actions,
the robe of this physical body is obtained.

By His Grace, 'Gate of Liberation' is opened wide
Which makes our faces shine in the spirit of self-confidence.

‼ Naanak Eveai Jaanee-ai Sabh Aapay Sachiaar ‼
The noble thoughts appearing at this ambrosial time
and putting them into practice open the doors for us
to finally embrace 'The Beloved One'. Says Nanak.

It is only then when we come to realize the truth,
that the 'Patient' the 'Doctor' and the 'Savior'
are all the one and same spiritually.

!! Step Fifth !!

(God, Truth and Message of Oneness)

we are all children of One and the Same God.
One God, One Religion, One Faith
Is what the words of
Love and Truth finally portray.

Yes, Interfaith is our Faith
where all the doors of our heart
are open to all shades of the people.

Virtues like that of Truth, Love, Kindness,
Compassion and Forgiveness
are not the monopoly of
some people or a group,
They are Universal.

The 'Invisible' can be very well
observed and realized by looking into
the eyes of an innocent when he feels
totally hopeless and cries for help.

!! Thaapi-aa Na jaa-ay Kee<u>t</u>aa Na Ho-ay !!
He cannot be established.

He cannot be created.
He cannot be changed by force.
He works by Himself.
And stays permancntly at peace.

!! Aapay Aap Niranjan So-ay !!
He Himself is Immaculate and Pure.
Like a lotus flower of the pond,
He stays unattached with all kinds of
negativities of life.

He keeps cool and maintains His Grace,
Dignity and Self-Respect
for all the times.

!! Jin Sayvi-aa tin Paa-i-aa Maan !!
Those who serve Him are honored.
They get the blessings of serving humanity
and in turn get themselves served gracefully.

!! Nanak Gaavee-ai Gunee NiDhaan !!
Says Nanak, those who listen Him, sing Him
and serve Him with devotion, have only earned
His Goodwill and become rich,
both materially and spiritually.

!! Gaavee-ai Sunee-ai Man Rakhee-ai Bhaa-o !!
He who listens and sings Him
through the sweet melody of His nature
and keeps his mind filled with
His Fear and Love
and works to His Will definitely crosses
the deadly ocean of this Earthly World.

!! Dukh Parhar Sukh Ghar Lai Jaa-ay !!
Performing such Noble Deeds,
one throws away all kinds of worries
which haunt him even when he is in sleep.

And at the same time that man with his
'Divine thoughts and Noble deeds'
brings everything most valuable close to him.

**!! Gurmukh NaadaN Gurmukh VaydaN
Gurmukh Rahi-aa Samai !!**
Guru's Word is the Sound-current of the Naad.
Guru's Word is the Wisdom of the Vedas.
Guru's Word is all-pervading.

The wisdom of Guru is 'Amrit' the nectar
and that nectar is spread in every gene of body of
those who remember Him, chant Him and act
in the way He acts.

Yes, simple living and high thinking
is finally His Command
to peace and progress.

!! Gur Eesar Gur Gorakh Barmaa Gur Paarbatee Maa-ee !!
Gobind, the God
Gorkh, the yogi
Brahman, the knower of both
the material and spiritual worlds,
Parvti, the wife of Shivji,
all are manifestations of
'One' and the same
'Holiest of the Holy Spirit'.

Everyone in fact looks differently
in his outer shell
but inside it is only Him.

!! Jay Ha-o Jaanaa Aakhaa Naahee Kahnaa Kathan Na Jaa-ee !!
Even knowing God, I cannot describe Him,
because He cannot be described in words.

No one can make Him understand to others too
by mere talking, teaching, preaching
or by use of force against His Will.

!! Guraa Ik Dayhi Bujhaa-ee !!
!! Sabhnaa Jee-aa Kaa Ik Daataa So Mai Visar Na Jaa-ee !!

Yes, but The Guru has most unambiguously
given me one understanding
that God, our father is One
and we are all His children.
May I ever remember Him looking into
the eyes of every being around.

!! Step Sixth !!

(Duality and Unanimity of Mind)

Yes, one and only one key is enough
to open the doors of all the three worlds.

Yes, only one virtue is enough
to open all the doors
of our heart and head
to realize Him.

If our Beloved, is not happy
due to one reason or the other,
what finally we achieve
bathing at the holy places?

!! Tirth Nava Je Tis Bhava Bin Bhane kii naae kri !!
Pleasing the Master, our Kant,
is the pilgrimage of
all the pilgrimages
and the Holy Bath.

Cleaning and decorating everything
without pleasing Him,
is just a ritual good for nothing.

!! Jeti Sirth Upaii Vekha Bin Karman ki Milaie Laii !!
Gazing all created beings without karma of good actions,
is only the blind rat race, revolving around the bush.

It is just firing the shots into darkness
wasting time, talent and treasure for nothing
other than the false pride of appearing better than others.

What ultimately are we going to receive,
if not the inner peace and tranquility.

The sum total and the essence of 'Spirit of Truth' therefore
is that anything earned by dubious and corrupt means
and politics of greed, is a mirage,
an illusion which finally vanishes away
in the blink of an eye right here in front of us
when the Master within is not pleased and at peace.

!! Mat Vich Ratan Javahar Maanik Je Ik Gur Ki Sikh Sunee !!
Gems and jewels are embedded
Well in our minds.
These can be easily explored and obtained
When we listen to Guru's Teachings,
And practice them truthfully.

The good seeds sown
with love and kindness
do produce beautiful flowers
and sweet fruits.

Yes, my dear,
even one good virtue if practiced religiously
will produce innumerous similar virtues.

if our children are good,
we don't need much of the material wealth.
They will be able to make it by themselves.
May be even better than we, the parents.

If our children finally turn out to be crooks,
we don't need much of the material wealth.
They will eat up everything
right here in front of our eyes.

!! Guraa Ik Dayhi Bujhaa-ee.!!
!! Sabhnaa Jee-aa Kaa Ik Dataa So Mai Visar Na Jaa-ee !!
Yes, but The Guru has most unambiguously given me
one understanding that God, our father is One
and we are all His children.
May I ever remember Him
looking into the beautiful eyes of every being.

!! Step Seventh !!

(Essence of His Grace and Blessings)

Wonderful and Priceless are His Countless Blessings my friend,
just watch how He works by itself in Synchronizing and
Supporting different organs of body to keep us alive.

Yes, whomsoever He bestows His Grace
Becomes King of all the Kings.

!! Jay Jug Chaaray Aarjaa Hor Dasoo<u>n</u>ee Ho-ay !!
Living throughout four ages,
or even ten times more does not matter.
What really matters is not how many times
someone visited Taj-Mahal in life.

What finally counts is what we finally
we achieved at the end of the day
if not peace and sound sleep.

!! Navaa K<u>h</u>anda Vich Jaa<u>n</u>ee-ai Naal Chalai Sa<u>bh</u> Ko-ay !!
Even if we are known throughout the nine continents
and followed by all because of our name and fame,
nothing sticks to us other than the virtues
which He, our 'Kant' likes.

!! Changa Naa-o Rakhaa-ay kai Jas keerat Jag lay-ay.
With a good name, fame and reputation.
With praise and fame throughout the world
and amongst all the four different categories of
species on and around the Earth,
What good is it that we cannot even understand
as to what really is good or bad for us
at the end of the day?

!! Jay Tis Nadar Na Aavee Ta Vaat Na Puchhai Kay !!
If the Lord does not bless us
with His Glance of Grace,
then who finally cares?

!! Kita Andr Kit Kar Dosi Dos Dharay !!.
Among worms, He will consider us like worms of a drain.
Even contemptible sinners would hold us in contempt
and very quickly stamp us the dirty worm of drain.

!! Naanak Nirgun Gun Kare Gunvantia Gun Day !!
Says Nanak,
God blesses unworthy with virtue,
and bestows virtue on the virtuous.

!! Teha Ko-ay Na Sujh-ee Je Tis Gun Koay Karay !!
No one can even imagine anyone
who can bestow virtue upon Him.
He only is the source of bestowing
all the virtues in everyone who trust Him.

!! Step Eighth !!

(Significance of Attentive Listening)

Listening attentively and peacefully
to the voice of soul within
and of the people around,
most of conflicts get resolved by itself.
Suffering and sin get destroyed.
The fear of death vanishes.

!! Su<u>n</u>i-ai Si<u>Dh</u> Peer Sur Naath !!
Listening the Holy Word,
we attain the wisdom of siddhas,
the spiritual teachers, the heroic warriors,
the yogic masters and many more.

Mere listening without attention is not suffice.
If the message is not correctly understood
and practiced in day to day life,
everything is a wastage of time
for both the speaker and the seeker.

!! Su<u>n</u>i-ai <u>Dh</u>arat Dhaval Aakaas !!
Listening sermons just ritualistically
about mother Earth, its support,

Ethers in universe and the galaxies
is not going to make much difference.
People have listened it throughout their lives.

!! Su<u>n</u>i-ai Deep lo-a Paa<u>t</u>aal !!
Listening the Holy Word,
We can envision vastness of oceans,
the lands and the Ghost Regions
of the underworld.

!! Su<u>n</u>i-ai Pohi Na Sakai Kaal !!
Death is dreadful and horrifying
until its meaning is spiritually understood
and the reality accepted in its
letter and spirit.

Listening the holy word
We become immortal.

!! Naanak B<u>h</u>ag<u>t</u>aa Sa<u>d</u>aa Vigaas !!
The devotees are forever in bliss.
And every day for them becomes a 'Spring'
Which they celebrate every day.

!! Su<u>n</u>i-ai Doo<u>kh</u> Paap Kaa Naas !!
Listening attentively the word of wisdom,
and practicing it truthfully,
pain and sin are erased
and our faces shine like the Sun.

!! Step Ninth !!

(Significance of Attentive Listening)

Listening attentively and peacefully,
even One of His Virtues,
Yoga of controlling mind
is best exercised.
It helps us understand
all the inner secrets of
our body and mind.

!! Su<u>n</u>i-ai Eesar Barmaa Ind !!
Listening attentively the Voice of Soul,
the prophets like, Shiva, Brahman and Indra
reach the heights of wisdom of Creator.

!! Su<u>n</u>i-ai Mu<u>kh</u> Saalaaha<u>n</u> Mand !!
Listening the Holy Word, even foul-mouthed people
praise Him and become sane and self-disciplined.

!! Su<u>n</u>i-ai Jog Juga<u>t</u> Tan B<u>h</u>ayd !!
Listening the Holy Word,
the technology of Yoga and secrets of body,
we can very well handle and discipline both,
to some extent better than outdoor exercises.

!! Suni-ai Saasat Simrit Vayd !!
Listening the Holy Word, we understand,
adjust and surmount the level of idle philosophy
and attain the wisdom of Shaastras,
Simritees and the Vedas.

!! Naanak Bhagtaa Sadaa Vigaas !!
The devotees are forever in bliss.
And every day for them becomes a 'Spring'
Which they celebrate every day.

!! Suni-ai Dookh Paap Kaa Naas !!
Listening attentively the word of wisdom,
and practicing it truthfully,
pain and sin are erased
and our faces shine like the Sun.

!! Step Tenth !!

(Significance of Attentive Listening)

Listening attentively and peacefully,
The voice of our soul within,
our mind gets stabilized
in the state of Equipoise,
the Everlasting Bliss.

!! Suni-ai Sat Santokh Giaan !!
Listening attentively the Voice of Soul,
our mind gets fully enlightened
with the invaluable virtues of Truth,
Contentment and Faith.

In that light we can clearly view and weigh
our strengths and weaknesses
and resolve conflicts amicably
without using force,
saving human lives and an
unimaginable loss of property.

Yes, where lies the peace,
there lies the progress, is the universal truth.

!! Sunia Athsath Ka Ishnan !!
Peace achieved through correct understanding of
spirit of truth in any given situation
and set of circumstances,
is better than ishnan (Bath)
at hundreds of holy places.

No one is born bad.
It is the situation and set of circumstances
surrounding everyone that makes one bad.

!! Suni-ai Parh Parh Paavahi Maan !!
Listening the Holi Word
reading and reciting,
honor is obtained.

Practice only makes the man perfect.
Reading and cramming volumes of books
and practicing nothing is just a hypocrisy,
the polished and projected face
and not the truth.

!! Suni-ai Laagai Shij Dhian!!
The attention fixed at the Holi Word
brings us to the 'State of Equipoise'
where in the Great Guru Arjun Dev JI
recited the words "Sweet is Thy Will"
even at the time of sitting at the hot iron sheet.

!! Naanak Bhagtaa Sadaa Vigaas !!
The devotees are forever in bliss.
And every day for them becomes a 'Spring'
Which they celebrate every day.

!! Su<u>n</u>i-ai Doo<u>kh</u> Paap Kaa Naas !!
Listening attentively the word of wisdom,
and practicing it truthfully,
pain and sin are erased
and our faces shine like the Sun of the sky.

!! Step Eleventh !!

(Significance of Attentive Listening)

Listening Attentively and peacefully
the voice of Soul within,
The blinds can cross the traffics safe.
And the deaf and dumb
can read Gita to others.

!! Suni-ai Saraa Gunaa Kay Gaah !!
Listening and diving deep into the ocean of virtues,
wealth of both the worlds is achieved.

!! Suni-ai Saykh Peer Paatisaah !!
Listening the Holy Word
Wisdom of Shaykhs, religious scholars,
spiritual teachers and emperors is achieved.

!! Suni-ai Andhay Paavahi Raahu !!
Listening the Holy Word even the ignorant and the blind
find the very short, straight and convenient way
to the Holiest of the Holy.

!! Su<u>n</u>i-ai Haath Hovai Asgaahu !!
Listening the Holy Word,
unreachable comes within reach.
Self-confidence is restored.

!! Naanak B<u>h</u>ag<u>t</u>aa Sa<u>d</u>aa Vigaas !!
The devotees are forever in bliss.
And every day for them becomes a 'Spring'
Which they celebrate every day.

!! Su<u>n</u>i-ai Doo<u>kh</u> Paap Kaa Naas !!
Listening attentively the word of wisdom,
and practicing it truthfully,
pains and sins are erased
and our faces shine like the Sun of the sky.

!! Step Twelfth !!

(Truthful acceptance of Holy Word)

Focusing, fixing and applying
the strengths of soul within,
even one good person like Nelson Mandela
can liberate his country from the slavery
of a big oppressive kingdom.

Listening and honoring the Holy Word,
mind gets perfectly clean and transparent.
The Blissful and Ecstatic state so achieved
cannot be described in words.

Truth and Love' are not three fourth,
half or a quarter pure and clean,
They are Unequivocally and Perfectly,
Pure and Clean.

!! Mannay Kee Ga<u>t</u> Kahee Na Jaa-ay !!
Listening intuitively,
reading and reciting Holy Word,
the Seeker is reborn into "Kingdom of God"

!! Jay Ko Kahai Pichhai Pachhutaa-ay !!

One who tries to explain the change of re-birth,
shall regret the attempt
because the change is total,
not quarter, half or three fourth.

!! Kaagad Kalam Na Likhanhaar !!

No pen can scribe enough on the paper,
people and prophets have written
volumes and volumes of books.

!! Mannay Kaa Bahi Karan Veechaar !!

The change of total attitude in human personality
gave birth to the process of sitting amicably
and resolving conflicts through dialogue
rather than use of force and authority
to change other's perceptions
and convictions.

!! Aisaa Naam Niranjan Ho-ay !!

Such is the state of Immaculate Lord
and such are His Attributes,
listening and practicing whom,
'The Faithful' becomes totally clean
from dualities and illusions of life
because of the total change
in the very gene of every cell of body.

!! Jay Ko Man Jaanai Man Ko-ay !!

Cleanliness and purity of body and mind,
Un-attachments from every kind of unworthy stuff,
is the hallmark of Immaculate Lord.

'The Faithful' can achieve those heights of glory
only when he is first mentally prepared
to sincerely follow the Immaculate Lord.

!! Step Thirteenth !!

(Truthful acceptance of Holy Word)

Listening and honoring Truth,
one gets enlightened about the self
and both the worlds of matter and spirituality.

!! Mannai Sura<u>t</u> Hovai Man Budh !!
The faithful develops intuitive awareness and intelligence
about the Universe and the 'Spirit of Truth'
This works to stabilize
and balance the Eco-System.

!! Mannai Sagal B<u>h</u>ava<u>n</u> Kee Sudh !!
The faithful knows about all the Realms
of both Matter and Spirituality.

!! Mannai Muhi Chotaa Naa K<u>h</u>aa-ay !!
The Faithful will never get slapped at the face
with the blows of dualities of mind.

!! Mannai Jam Kai Saath Na Jaa-ay !!
The faithful does not have to go
with the Messenger of Death.
Knowledge of truth and reality

replaces the fear of death
into the "State of Ecstasy",
the "State of Celebration".

The faithful at that time no more remains
an object to be used and abused by others.

He becomes "Observer" to observe and enjoy
the play of dolls and the circus
of this transitionary world.

!! Aisaa Naam Niranjan Ho-ay !!
Such is the state of Immaculate Lord
and such are His Attributes,
listening and practicing whom,
'The Faithful' becomes totally clean
from dualities and illusions of life
because of the total change
in the very gene of every cell of body.

!! Jay Ko Man Jaanai Man Ko-ay !!
Cleanliness and purity of body and mind,
Un-attachments from every kind of unworthy stuff,
is the hallmark of Immaculate Lord.

'The Faithful' can achieve those heights of glory
only when he is first mentally prepared
to sincerely follow up the Immaculate Lord.

!! Step Fourteenth !!

(Truthful acceptance of Holy Word)

Listening, understanding its essence and honoring the Holy Word
We get attached to Him directly rather than working through
His agents like the teachers, preachers, pastors
and professors of comparative study of religions.

Realizing clearly that God and Truth is One
we no more wander and follow so many
useless and unproductive rituals in our day to day life.

!! Mannai Maarag Thaak Na paa-ay !!
The path of the faithful shall never be blocked.
it becomes very simple and straight
as he has thrown away all kinds of garbage
which usually keeps him enslaved
into the cages of doubts
and dualities of mind.

!! Mannai Pat si-o Pargat Jaa-ay !!
The faithful, wherever he is
and whatever he is

shall depart with honor and fame.
He becomes totally independent
from the effects of Time and Space.

Spiritually He becomes a citizen of the world.
whole of humanity and creation
becomes his family and faith.

!! Mannai Mag Na Chalai Panth !!
The faithful does not believe to follow the path of
empty religious rituals and usel formalities.

The way to life for him becomes only one,
straightway of Divine Truth
Which he never wavers to follow.

He saves every hard-earned penny
From wherever he can
and spends it he must.

!! Mannai Dharam Saytee San-BanDh !!
The faithful gets by itself attached to only one faith,
The undying faith directly with the 'Lord of Lords'
the religion of love, kindness, compassion
and Universal Brotherhood.

No other organized, created
or man-made religion in-between.

!! Aisaa Naam Niranjan Ho-ay !!
Such is the state of Immaculate Lord
and such are His Attributes,
listening and practicing whom,
'The Faithful' becomes totally clean
from dualities and illusions of life

because of the total change
in the very gene of every cell of the body.

!! Jay Ko Man Jaanai Man Ko-ay !!
Cleanliness and purity of body and mind,
Un-attachments from every kind of unworthy stuff,
is the hallmark of Immaculate Lord.

'The Faithful' can achieve those heights of glory
only when he is first mentally prepared
to sincerely follow up the Immaculate Lord.

!! Step Fifteenth !!

(Truthful acceptance of Holy Word)

Listening, understanding its essence and honoring Truth
with logic and reasoning, the Believer along with him,
streers so many others too along with him
out of the whirl winds of deadly sea.

!! Mannai Paavhi Mokh Duaar !!
The Faithful finds the door of liberation
from all kind of fears, worries and pains
and for all the times.

!! Mannai Parvaarai Saadhar !!
Not only himself alone, the Faithful uplifts and redeems
his family, friends and relations too
and makes them the inhabitants of
the "Kingdom of God'

!! Mannai Tarai Taarai Gur Sikh !!
So many others like him too get liberated with Faithful,
the way our sixth Guru did in liberating fifty-two helpless kings.

!! Mannai Nanak Bhavahi Na Bhikh !!
Says Nanak,

The believer and worshiper of the beauty and strength
never becomes so weak to beg, waive or surrender
to the dark forces of distress and depression.

!! Aisaa Naam Niranjan Ho-ay !!

Such is the state of Immaculate Lord
and such are His Attributes,
listening and practicing whom,
'The Faithful' becomes totally clean
from all kinds of dualities and illusions of life,
because of the total change
in the very gene of every blood cell of the body.

!! Jay Ko Man Jaanai Man Ko-ay !!

Cleanliness and purity of body and mind,
Un-attachments from every kind of unworthy stuff,
is the hallmark of Immaculate Lord.

'The Faithful' can achieve those heights of glory
only when he is first mentally prepared
to sincerely follow up the Immaculate Lord.

!! Step Sixteenth !!

(Principal of Consensus and Unanimity)

Principal of 'Consensus and Unanimity'
is the Law of Nature,
is the Principal of
'Social Self-Discipline'
Commendable !

<u>Our Earth does not hang on the horn of
a big bull as some orthodox people
used to believe in olden days.</u>

<u>Universe is following "The Laws of Nature'
and supported by itself as proved by the
'Law of Conservation of Energy',
the 'Law of Forces' and many other laws.
It maintains its balance by itself.</u>

<u>This validates nothing but the spirit of
all Prevailing Truth'</u>

!! Panch Parvaa<u>n</u> Panch Pard<u>h</u>aan !!
The chosen ones, the self-elect having full control
over the five ghosts of lust, anger, greed,

over attachment and ego are accepted
and approved in His court.

!! Panchay Paavahi Dargahi Maan !!
The chosen ones are honored in the Court of Lord.
In the universe of 'Truth and Love',
spirit of dialogue, understanding and consensus
is considered economical, productive
and human rather than use of force.

!! Panchay Sohahi Dar Raajaan !!
The chosen ones filled with
nectar of sublime essence,
look beautiful in the courts of kings.

!! Panchaa Kaa Gur ek Dhiaan !!
Chosen with consensus work with consensus
Not with dictatorship or politics of voting
They always stay focused on Him.

Hundreds of the wise have
the same sacred mission, same focus
and work in same direction
Whereas hundreds of fools
have countless of their own
selfish motives at their back.

!! Jay Ko Kahai Karai veechaar !!
No matter how much anyone tries to explain
and describe Him, He cannot be known
and expressed in words.

!! Kartay Kai Karnai Naahee Sumaar !!
Actions of Creator
Can also not be Counted

Measured or Weighed
on any scale.

!! Dhoul Dharam Daya Kaa Poot !!.
The mythical bull on whose horn
Earth is supposed to be pivoted is Dharma,
the son of kindness and compassion.

!! Santokh Thaap Rakhiaa Jin Soot !!
Kindness, compassion and contentment
is what patiently holds the Earth
in its balance and its place.

!! Jay Ko Bujhai Hovai Sachiaar !!
One who understands
this phenomenon of nature
becomes truthful.

!! Dhavlai Upar Kaytaa Bhaar !!
What a great load there is
on the established fictional bull,
no one can even imagine.

!! Dhartee Hor Parai Hor Hor !!
So many worlds beyond this world
countless in number.

We are born not to spend our life
only to raise some victory flags
and invite all the time anxiety,
the source of hidden stress
rather than fixing peace
as the driver of engine.

!! Tis Tay Bhaar Talai Kavan Jor !!.
Not known what power holds them,
and supports their weight
Un-Knowable mystery !

!! Jee-a Jaat Rangaa Kay Naav !!
Countless are the names,
the colors and classes of
assorted species of beings.

!! Sabhnaa Likhi-aa Vurhee Klaam !!
Everything was inscribed
by the Ever-flowing Pen of God
and that too in just a blink of an eye.

!! Eh Lekha Likh Jaanai Koe !!
Who knows how to write this account?
He is Endless and Endless is His account.

!! Lekha Likhia Keta Hoe !!
Just imagine what a huge scroll His account would take.
The scroll increases as it goes further because
He 'The Scroll Writer' is endless.
And the Universe is Endless.

!! Kita Taan Suaaliu Roop !!
What power He possesses?
What fascinating beauty is
His whole personality?
In-Expessible !

!! Kete Daat Jaane Kaun Koot !!
What gifts and who can
know their value content?
Marvellous !

!! Kita Psaao Eko Kvao !!
He created the vast expanse of Universe
with just One Word!

!! Tis Te hoe Lakh Driao !!
Hundreds of thousands of rivers
then began to flow by itself!

!! Kudrt Kvn Kha Vichar !!
How can His Creative Potency
be described?
No-Way!

!! Varia Na Java ek var !!!
Not Even once o' God
I can be a sacrifice to YOU.

!! Jo Tudh Bhavai Saii Bhli Kar !!
Whatever pleases YOU
is the only good done.

!! Tu Sda Slaamt Nirankar !!
May the Eternal and Formless One
stay forever is my prayers!

!! Step Seventeenth !!

(Essence of His Grace and Blessings)

Not even once O' God,
I can be sacrifice to YOU.
The Expanse of your
Grace and Blessings is Unthinkable.

Japi, tapi, jati, sati, moni, yogi, gods,
donors, devotees and heroes are countless.
Everyone prays you for the gifts of
Your Kindness, Forgiveness and Blessings.

!! Aasankh Jap Aasankh Bhaa-o !!
Countless are the meditators,
the creatures who sing YOU non-stop.
And love YOU from the core of their hearts.

!! Aasankh Poojaa Asankh Tap taa-o !!
Countless worship YOU treating YOU
solely as their own and work hard
maintaining strict Austere Disciplines.

!! Asankh Garanth Mukh Ved Paath !!
Countless are the scriptures

and ritual recitations of the Vedas
in YOUR name.

!! Asan<u>kh</u> Jog Man Rahahi U<u>d</u>aas !!
Countless are the Yogis,
whose minds remain detached
from the world and as such
they remain always sad
and finally return back as did Budha,
and finally accepted YOU and YOUR WILL

!! Asankh Bhgat Gun Gian Vichar !!
Countless are the devotees who contemplate
YOUR wisdom and virtues
and wish enjoy YOUR company always,
as did Mardanan, the soul mate of Nanak.

Asankh Sti Asankh Asakh Datar !!
Countless are the Holy Sages.
Countless are the Astatics
who renunciate this material world
and hide in the mountains.

Countless are the givers
Like Satyavadi Harish Chandra,
who donated everything
in YOUR name
neglecting their basic Dharma of
serving even his wife and son.

!! Asankh Sur Muhn Bhakh Saar !!
Countless are the heroic spiritual warriors,
who bear the brunt of attacks
straight at their faces
and sacrifice their lives

fulfilling their duty and responsibility
to please YOU.
!! Asankh Mon Liv Lae Taar !!
Countless are the silent sages,
vibrating the String of YOUR LOVE
and stay all the time focused on YOU.

!! Kudrat Kvn Khaa Vichar !!
How can
YOUR CREATIVE POTENCY
be described?
Impossible to express
and put something
in black and white!

!! Varia Na Java ek var !!
Not Even once O' God
I can be a sacrifice to YOU.

!! Jo Tudh Bhavai Saii Bhli Kar !!
Whatever pleases YOU
is the only good done.

!! Tu Sda Slaamt Nirankar !!
May the Eternal and Formless One
stay forever is my prayers!

!! Step Eighteenth!!

(God, His Nature and His Creation)

Infinite sin is the attitude of some people
They constantly sin and earn the punch of
sinful deeds on their heads.

May God forgive them
and bless them too with good luck !

!! Asankh Murkh Andh Ghor !!
Countless are the fools,
blinded by ignorance,
they all the time complain, criticize,
curse and fault faults in others.

!! Aslakh Chor Hraam khoor !!
Countless are the thieves and embezzlers
who never work other than to steel,
deceive and bluff others.

!! Asankh Amar Kr Jae Jor !!
Countless are those
who simply impose
their Will on others.

Hook or by crook
they please themselves
using and abusing them.

!! Asankh Gal Vadh Huttia Kmae !!
Countless cut-throats,
the ruthless killers
having no element of
kindness or compassion
even for themselves and their children.

!! Asankh Papi Pap Kr Jae !!
Countless are the sinners,
who keep on sinning
all through their lives.

!! Asankh Kudiar Kude Firahe !!
Countless are the liars,
wandering lost in the world of lies,
nothing else to do other than to
enjoy gossip and slander as their hobby.

!! Asankh Malechh Mal BHKH Khae !!
Countless are the wretches,
eating filth as their food and ration.
Like the worm of a drain,
they have developed the taste only for filth.
They therefore live and die in the drains.

!! Asankh Nindak Sir Karhi Bhar !!
Counless are the slanderers
carrying the weight of
their stupid mistakes on their heads.

Nanak Neech Kahai Vichar !!
Says Nanak, the humblest of the humble,
such is the state of these
gossip mongerers, liers and slanderers.

!! Varia Na Java ek var !!
Not Even once O' God
I can be a sacrifice to YOU.

!! Jo Tudh Bhavai Saii Bhli Kar !!
Whatever pleases YOU
is the only good done.

!! Tu Sda Slaamt Nirankar !!
May the Eternal and Formless One
stay forever is my prayers.

!! Step Nineteenth !!

(Significance of the letter 'Word' in Language)

The letter 'Word' is the first and the last means
of communication used in language.
It is used to communicate, understand
and work with each other.

How wonderful and mystic this very thought is,
to even think that there is no such word
written on the forehead of Creator!

Blessed is the wordless thought of Creator
and blessed is His 'Wordless Truth'

!! Asnnkh Nam Asankh Thaav !!
Countless are the names of
countless places in Universe,
which we may like to visit and enjoy
in this very short span of life.

!! Agam Agam Asankh loaa !!
There are countless inaccessible and unapproachable
Celestial Realms in this Universe

which we may like to invent and explore
in this short span of life.

!! Asankh khai Sir Bhaar Hoie !!
Even to call them countless,
is to carry the weight on our head.
It makes us a bit more uncomfortable.

!! Akhri Nam Akhri Salaah !!
From the word comes the name.
From the word comes the praise.
With the word world wars started
With the word compromises made
With the word forgiveness is exercised.

But word too is not perfect.
Word is just the means to express thought.
It only is the practice of Truth
which finally works and counts.

!! Akhri Gian Geet Gun Gaah !!
From the word comes spiritual wisdom,
singing the songs of His Glory.
Honoring the promises and commitments
Is the way to Peace. Truth and Life.

.

!! Akhri Likhan Bolan Baan !!
Through the words only, we speak,
write, sing and make others to
understand as to what really
we mean.

!! Akhri Sir Sanjog vkhaan !!
From the word

we make and break relationships.
From the word comes the destiny
written on forehead.

!! Jin Eh Likhai Tise Sir Naahi !!
<u>But the one who wrote these words,
Himself has no such word on His forehead.</u>
He simply is guided only by His sweet will.

!! Jiv Furmaae Tiv Tiv Paaie !!
As He ordains through our soul,
so do we receive.
Yes, but the communicator and the recipient
may not be at the same wave length.

Here comes the conflict.
Here comes divorce.
And here comes
all kinds of divisive politics.

!! Jeta Keeta Teta Hoie !!
The Universe is manifestation of His name.
Whatever seeds of 'Action'
a farmer sows in field
same shall he receive in return.

No one can avoid or change the figure and facts
written in the wordless language of Karma.
This is the 'Law of Nature'.

!! Vin Nava Nahi Ko Thaao !!
There is no other choice,
no other place other than His Will.
Sowing the seeds of poison and ill will,
We cannot expect nectar and His Love.

!! Kudrt Kvn Kha Vichar !!
How can
YOUR CREATIVE POTENCY
be described?
No way!

!! Varia Na Java ek var !!!
Not Even once O' God
I can be a sacrifice to YOU.

!! Jo Tudh Bhavai Saii Bhli Kar !!
Whatever pleases YOU
is the only good done.

!! TU Sda Samt Nirnkar !!
May the Eternal and Formless one
Stay forever in my prayers.

!! Step Twentieth !!

(Sinful Thoughts and Their Liberation)

Liberation from sinful thoughts
can only be achieved
by working to His Will
and practicing what we preach.

This only pleases Him, the 'Kant'
sitting at the core of our heart.

!! Bharie Hth Pair Tn Khehi !!
When the hands, the feet
and the body are dirty.

!! Pani Dhote Utrs Khehi !!
Washing with water,
most of the dirt
can be easily washed away.

!! Muut Pleeti Kapad Hoie !!
If the clothes are soiled
and stained by urine.

!! De Sabun Laie Oh Dhoe !!
These clothes can be wash cleaned

with soap and other such
disinfectants.

!! Bhrie Mtt Papan Ke Sng !!
But when the intellect is stained
and polluted by sin.

!! Oh Dhopai Nava Ke Rng !!
It can only be cleaned by
Love and blessings of Lord.
No short cuts!

!! Punee Papi Aakhn Nahi !!
Virtue and vice do not come by mere
words of praise or disrespect.

Truth is always perfected
by practice of good deeds.

!! Kr Kr Krnan Likh Lai Jahu !!
Actions repeated over and over again
are engraved on the Soul.
Mere teaching or preaching of sermons
from a Holy Book is just a hypocrisy
of the worst kind.

!! Aape Bij AApe Hi Khahu !!
We will harvest only what we plant.
This is the 'Law of Nature'.
This is His will.

The seeds of good quality flowers
and plants planted today
will surely deliver beautiful flowers
and sweet fruits for tomorrow.

!! Nanak Hukmi Aavhu Jaavhu !!
By the Hukam of God' command,
We come and go, we sleep and awake,
we gain or lose.

This is the outcome of everything
we practically performed till yesterday.

!! Step Twenty First !!

(Re-birth in the state of Equipoise)

Taking holy baths at the places of pilgrimages
to clean body and mind are useless,
if our Beloved, sitting at the very core of
our heart is not pleased.
Liberation from sins
is only achieved
by practicing His will.

!! Tirth Tap Daya Dat Daan !!
The Pilgrimages, austere discipline,
compassion and charity
are the means not the end.

Following all the above disciplines
may or may not lead us to the
desired destination of "Ultimate Bliss'

The needle of mind comes back
to the same situation of helplessness.
It happened with Budha and so many
other seekers and explorers of Truth.

!! Je Ko Pavai Til Ka Maan !!

Following all the above disciplines,
even if someone achieves something,
that something is worth nothing
rather than wastage of time,
talent and treasure.

!! Sunie Mnnie Man Kita Bhau !!

Listening and believing with love and humility
Definitely bring us closer to Our Beloved
but not really with the Beloved.

Deep Devotion and Dedication only
is the trustable bond.

!! Antargti Tirath Mal Naao !!

Cleaning our mind
with the spirit of righteousness
and virtues dearer to our Beloved,
is only the way to the Lord
we seek to be with.

!! Sabh Gun Tere Mai Nahi Koay !!

All virtues pertain to Lord,
I have none.
Even the next breath
is not in my control.

!! Vin Gun Kitai Bhagat Na Hoay !!

Without virtue, there is no devotional worship.
Without practically following virtues,
the Lord is not pleased and
everything turns out to be a mere waste.

!! Suast Aath Bani Burmao !!
I bow to the Lord,
The Blissful and Liberator from Ego
His Word is True, the Brahman.

!! Sat Suhaan Sda Man Chaao !!
He, The Lord is Beautiful,
True and Eternally Joyful.

!! Kavan So Velaa Vkt Kavan Kavan Thiti Kanan Var !!
What was that time and moment?
What was that day and date
when He made His presence
here in the Universe?

!! Kavan Si Rutti Maah Kavan Jit Hoaa Aakar !!
What was that season and the Month
When the Universe was created?

When were the sizes, shapes and colors
like the one appears in sky
in the form of a rainbow created?

!! Vail Na Paaiie Pandti Je Hovie Lekh Puran !!
The Pandits and religious scholars too
cannot find that time
even if it is written in Puranas.

!! Vakhut Naa Paiaa Kaadiaa Je Like Lekh Kuran !!
That time is not known
even to the Quazis
who study The Koran.

!! Thit Vaar Naa Jogi Janae Rut Maah Na Koie !!
Yogis too do not know the date, day,

the season and the month
when He converted Himself from One
which was colorless to varieties of
Color, Size and Shape'.

!! Ja Kartaa Shrishti Ko Saje Aape Jaane Soee !!
The Creator who created this creation,
only He Himself knows as to how
He created all this
in just one stretch
and split of a second.

!! Kiv Kar Aakhaa Kiv Saalahi Kiv Varnin Kiv Jaanan !!
How can we speak of Him?
How can we Praise Him?
How can we describe Him?
And how can we know Him?
Only He knows.

!! Nanak Aakhan Sabh Ko Aakhe Ikk Du Ikk Siaanan !!
Says Nanak, everyone speaks of Him
and considers himself wiser
and smarter than others.

!! Vadda Sahib Vadda Naaee Kita ja ka Hovai !!
Great is The Master,
Great is His Name.
Whatever happens
is according to His Will.

!! Nanak Je Ko Aapaou Janai Agai Giaa NaaSohaie !!
One who claims to know everything
shall not be decorated
in both the worlds hereafter.

!! Step Twenty Second !!

(Finite Can't Assess and Evaluate Infinite)

Limited senses of body cannot assess
and evaluate the 'Limitless'
That is why we simply pass the judgement
that He only knows Himself.

We just limit and reduce the Lord in us
to the capability and capacity of our limited sense
due to the ignorance of Truth and Ego
and then wander helplessly to seek Him
from somewhere outside!

!! Pataala Pataal Lakh Aagasa Aagaas !!
There are nether worlds beneath nether worlds,
and hundreds of thousands of heavenly worlds.
Everything is Endless and Limitless!
!! Odak Odak Bhal Thake Ved Khin Ikk Vaat !!
The Vedas say that we cannot search
for all of them until we grow weary.

!! Sehas Athaarah Khin Ktebaa Aslu Ikko Dhaat !!
The scriptures say that there are 18,000 worlds

but in reality there is only ONE UNIVERSE,
ONE GOD and ONE TRUTH.

!! Lekha Hoe Taa Likhiie Lekhe Hoay Vinaas !!
With the limited capacity of our intellect,
finite can never even comprehend infinite.
If we try to write an account
we will surely finish ourselves
before we finish the writing.

But Yes, we can do realize Him and be one with Him
through practicing the virtues and all good deeds.

!! Nanak Vadda Aakhie Aape Jaane Aap !!
Call Him Great says Nanak,
He Himself only knows Himself.
The tragedy here is that o' man
that we do not know ourselves
and that He very well lives in us.

!! Step Twenty Third !!

(Difference of Big and Small in Spiritual Sense)

We do praise and sing Him breathlessly and blindly
but don't necessarily understand Him
and comprehend His capacities and capabilities.

Like a river, who joins the sea
but knows very little about
the vastness of the Sea.

All the seekers of Truth
if clubbed together
cannot even equate to an ant
who understands Him
and works to His Will.

!! Saalahi Saalahe Etii Surt Na Paiie !!
The praisers praise the Lord
but they cannot obtain
His intuitive understanding.

!! Ndiaa atai Vaah pvahi Samund Na Jaanie !!
The streams and rivers
do merge into the ocean,

Following the Law of Nature
But not knowing anything about him.

We do live our lives
And finally go back to Him
But because of the Ego element
We stay detached from Him.

!! Samund Shah Sultaan Girhaa Seti Maal Dhan !!
Like Dhritrashtra of Mhan-Bhart,
The kings and emperors
with mountains of material wealth
do not matter Him
if they are not at peace
and pleased with themselves

!! Kiidi Tull Na Hovay Je Tis Mno Na visraie !!
Those kings and emperors are not equal to an ant.
They can't even look face to face with her
who keeps always attached to Him.

!! Step Twenty Fourth !!

(Praise of the Invisible All Powerful)

He only is Great.
He only is
'Time-less and Space-less'
He only understands and knows Him.

!! Ant Na Sifti Khin Na Ant !!
Endless are His Praises
Endless are those who speak Him.

!! Ant na Karnin Den Na Ant !!
Endless are His Actions.
Endless are His Gifts,
gifted un-conditionally.

!! Ant Na Vekhan Sunan Na Ant !!
Beyond galaxies is His Vision of Truth.
Immearable is His capacity of listening.
He looks at us and listens us
Even when we are alone
Locked in four walls of our room.

We listen His voice
Through every being,
bird and animal.

!! Ant Na Japaie Kia Man Mant !!
His limits cannot be perceived.
What really is the mystery
and what really He thinks
is un-knowable.

Difficult even to imagine as to
what type of Ramaynana
or Mhanbharta episodes
are emerging at the screen
of a human mind.

!! Ant Na Jaapai Kita Aakar !!
Limits of the created Universe,
The spirit of His Unity in Diversity
and Diversity in Unity
cannot be correctly perceived.

!! Ant Na Jaapai Paravar !!
Its limits here and beyond
cannot be perceived
with all five senses of our body.

!! Ant Kaarn Kete Billaie !!
Countless seekers of Truth
like Budha and so many others
have struggled to the point of break
but could not find anything significant.

!! Ta Ke Ant Na Pae Jahe !!
The limits and boundaries
of His capacity and capabilities
are un-markable.

!! Eho Ant Na Jaanen Koay !!
The end of His vision is incomprehensible
Because the height of The Great
is incomprehensible.

!! Bhuta Kahie Bhuta Hoay !!
The more we say about Him,
the more is there still to be said.

!! Vadda Sahib Vadda Ucha Thaao !!
The store of His 'Beauties and Virtues'
is unimaginably wide and bigger
than the limited capacity of our senses.
The place and level of His
'Thought and Action'
is too high to be measured.
On any scale.

!! Uche Upar Ucha Naao !!
Highest of High
And above all is His name.

!! Ayvad Ucha Hovaie Koay !!
One who achieves the greatness
and height as He is,
can only measure Him
and speak something about Him.

!! Tis Uche Kao Janan Soay !!
He only can know His
Lofty and Exalted State.

!! Jayvad Aap Janen Aap Aap !!
Only He Himself is that Great.
Only He Himself knows Himself.

!! Nanak Ndrii Karmin Daat !!
With His Glance of Grace only
Says Nanak,
He bestows His Blessings.

!! Step Twenty Fifth !!

(Uniqueness of His Blessings and way of Forgiveness)

Countless and invaluable are His Blessings
and countless are the blessed ones
who for all the time enjoy His Blessings
and with all that He does not seek any charity.

He does not complain, criticize, compare,
curse or find faults in others
just to claim His Supremacy,
He just ignores and overlooks
all such illusionary intuitions of mind
and moves further through His Prayers of
forgiveness for all those who sinned
because of their ignorance of Truth.

!! Bhuta Karam Likhia Na Jaae !!
So abundant is His work and blessings
that there can be no written account of them.

!! Vadda Daata Til Na Tam !!
He is the one and only one
Both as a Giver and Taker
At the same time

In whole of the universe,
Very open and big in His heart.

A giver and a taker are hands of one body
wherein blood from the same heart
flows in every vein.

!! Kete Mange Jodh Apaar !!
There are so many great, heroic warriors
begging at the door of the Infinite Lord.

!! Ketia Ganit Nahi Vichar !!
So many at the receiving end,
contemplate and dwell on Him
and cannot be counted.

!! Kete Khap Tutte Vekaar !!
So many waste their lives
engaged in corruption
and at the end find themselves helpless.

Budha, the researcher of peace,
spent whole of his life
to find 'Cause and Effect'
of old age disease and death
but in vein.
He finally reconciled
and realized the Truth of
working His Wiil. and feel at ease.

!! Kete Lai Lai Mukkar Paae !!
So many take and take again and then deny
whatever they unconditionally received.
The thankless and unworthy of trust.

!! Kete Murakh Khahee Khae !!
So many foolish consumers
keep on consuming charities
without taking any responsibility
of doing something for others.
Never ever they feel satisfied
and contented.

!! Ketia Dukh Bhukh Sad-Mar !!
So many endure distress,
deprivation and constant abuse.
They for all the time feel sad and bad
and never dare to take a stand
wherever it is called for.

!! Eh Bhi Daat Teri Dataar !!
These too are YOUR gifts O'God
because with these gifts
You are constantly trying to show them
their spotty faces in the mirror
and help them regain their lost strengths
due to long time habit of their
self-cultivated habits of beggary.

!! Band Khlasi Bhanan Hoe !!
Liberation from bondage comes only by His will
and one can awake again from his sleep of
laziness and lethargy.

!! Hor Aakh Na Ske Koe !!
No one else has any say in this gift of
deprivation blessed to the lazy.
There cannot perhaps be a better way
for their re-birth from the pitiable state
of their helplessness.

!! Je Ko khaaik Aakhn Pae !!
If some fool pressures to say that he does,
he cannot explain the phenomenon of
God's ways to effectively handle
such corrective measures.

!! Oh Jaane Jetia Muhn Khaae !!
He who speaks in support of
the self-made idlers
can only assess and observe
as to how many blows
he bears on his face.

!! Aape Janen Aape Day-ay !!
He Himself knows. He Himself takes
He Himself gives.
His ways of rejoicing are of His own
Very unique is His rule of the game.

!! Aakhe Se Bhi Kayee kayay !!
Very few are those who acknowledge
the rules of His game and follow them.

!! Jis Nuun Bakhshe Sifat Salaah !!
One who is blessed to sing His praises
is only capable of understanding
the reality of such situations.

!! Nanak Patshahi Patshah !!
He is only the King of Kings,
Says Nanak,
And He only is the One
An Evergreen Giver.

!! Step Twenty Sixth !!

(Praise of the Lord and His Creation)

Priceless are YOUR Attributes.
Very straight forward
and un-apologetic
is YOUR Command.
No one can express, explain and weigh
the value of YOUR Virtues.
If someone tries to express YOU,
he miserably fails.

!! Amul Gun Amul Amul Vapar !!
Priceless are the Vrtues embedded in YOU.
Priceless is YOUR Praise and "Sucha-Sauda",
The business profitable to everyone.

!! Amul Vaparie Amul Bhandar !!

Priceless are YOUR dealing of
Give and Take with others
And Priceless are the Dealers
doing business with YOU.
Priceless are YOUR Treasures
Which always stay filled.

!! Amul Aavhi Amul Lai Jaahi !!
Priceless are those who come to YOU
And do go away fully satisfied
And contented from YOUR doors.

!! Amul Bhaae Amula Smaae !!
Priceless is their Love for YOU
And priceless is the absorption in YOU
Peace and Peace all around.

!! Amul Dharm Amul Divaan !!
Priceless is His Divine Law of Dharma.
And priceless is YOUR court of justice.

!! Amul Tul Amul Parvaan !!
Priceless are YOUR scales of weighing.
And priceless are YOUR weights
With which YOU weigh.
Hand for hand
And head for Head.

.

!! Amul Bakhsheesh Amul Nissan !!
Priceless are YOUR blessings.
Priceless is the Banner and Insignia.

!! Amul Karm Amul Furmaan !!
Priceless is YOUR kindness and Mercy.
And Unique is YOUR Royal Command.

!! Amulo Amul Aakhia Na Jaae !!
Priceless is YOU my Beloved
Beyond words and expression.

!! Aakh Aakh Rhe Liv Laaie !!
Believers and Virtuous like to speak
about YOU my Lord
And like to remain
always absorbed in YOU.

!! Aakhhi Ved Paath Puraan !!
The Vedas and Puranas speak about YOU.
The Gita and Koranans speak about YOU.

!! Aakhhi Padeh Kre Vikhiaan !!
The scholars lecture day in and day out
and philosophers speak endlessly about YOU.

!! Aakhe Barma Aakhe Ind !!
Brahman speaks of YOU.
Indra speaks of YOU.

!! Aakhe Gopi Te Gobind !!
The Gopis and Krishnan
speaks of about YOU.

!! Aakhhi Eesar Aakhhi Sidh !!
Shiva and Sidhas
speaks of YOU

!! Aakhhi Kete Kaite Budh !!
So many of Budhas tried to know YOU
and explore YOU
But finally reconciled with YOU

!! Aakhhi Daanv Akhhi Dev !!
The demons speak about YOU.
And the demi-gods speak about YOU.

!! Aakhi Sur Nar Mun Jan Seyv !!
The spiritual warriors,
the heavenly beings,
the silent sages,
the humble and YOUR servants speak.

!! Kete Aakhhi Aakhn Paahi !!
Many speak and try to describe YOU.
And spoken Him endlessly.

!! Kete Khi Khi Uthth Uthth Jaaii !!
Over and over again
so many came and gone.
And awakened to Higher Consciousness.

!! Ayte Kite Hor Kare !!
YOU created as many again
as there already were.
Priceless Jewels of Virtus.

!! Ta Aakh Na Skai Koi Ke !!
Even then no one could
explain and express YOU.

!! Jayvad Bhaavai Tayvad Hoie !!
YOU become as great
as YOU wish to be.

!! Nanak Jaane Saacha Soie !!
Says Nanak,
Only the Truthful knows YOU.

!! Je Ko Aakhhi Bol Vigaad !!
If anyone presumes and claims
to describe YOU.

!! Ta Lkhie Sir Gaavara Gavaar !!
He shall be known
as the greatest fool of fools.

!! Step Twenty Seventh !!

(Praise of the Lord and His Creation)

Countless are those who for all the times
pray and praise for Him.
But the real and right one are those
who fully immerse and absorbe in Him.

!! So Dar Kayhaa So Ghar Katha Jit Bhi Sarab Smaale !!
Where is that gate and where is that dwelling,
in which He sits and take care of His Creation?

!! Vaje Naad Anek Asankha Kete Vaavanhare !!
The Sound current of Naad vibrates there
and countless musicians play on all sorts of
instruments there.

!! Kete Raag Prii Sio Kahiin Kete Gavanhare !!
So many Raagas
And so many musicians
singing there at His doors.

**!! Gavhi Tudh-No Paun Pani Baisantar
Gavai Raja Dharam Duaare !!**
The life-saving wind, water and fire sing.
The Righteous Judge of Dharma sing too.

!! Gavhi Chit Gupat Likhi Jaane Likh Likh Dharam Vichare !!
The angel of conscious and subconscious,
who record actions and the Righteous Judge of
Dharma who judges the record sing.

!! Gavhi Eesar Burma Devi Sohan Sdaa Svaare !!
Shiva, Brahman
and the Goddess of Beauty
ever adorned sing.

!! Gavhi Ind Idaasan Baithe Devtiaa Dar Nale !!
Indra seated upon His thrown sing
with deities at His door.

!! Gavhi Sidh Smadhi Andar Gaavni Sadh Vichare !!
The Sidhas in Samadhi sing,
The Sadhus sing in contemplation.

!! Gavan Jti Sti Sntokjii Gavan Tudhno Vir Krare !!
The celebates, the fanatics, the contented
and the fearless warriors sing.

!! Gavan Padit Padhan Rkhisar Jug Jug Veda Naale !!
The Padits, the religious scholars who recite Vedas
with the supreme sages of all ages sing.

!! Gavhi Mohnian Man Mohan Surga Machh Paaiale !!
The Mohinis, the enchanting heavenly beauties,
who entice hearts in this world,
sing in Vrindavan at the melodious tune
Of His Bansuri.

!! Gavan Rattan Upae Tere Ath Sath Tirath Naalae !!
The underworld of the sub conscious sing

The Celestial Jewels created by Him
And the sixty-eight places of pilgrimage sing.

!! Gaavhi Jodh Mhabal Sura Gaavhi Khaani Cgaare !!
The brave and mighty warrior sing.
The spiritual heroes and the four sources
of creation sing.

!! Gaavhi Knand Mandal Verbhadaa KarKar Rakhe Dhare !!
The planets, solar systems and galaxies,
created by His hand sing.

**!! Sayee Tudhno Gavan Jo Tudh Bhavan
Ratte Tere Bhagat Rsaale !!**
They alone sing, who are pleasing to Him.
His devotees are imbued
with the Nectar of His Essence.

!! Hori Kete Gavn Se Mai Chiti Na Aavni Nank Kia Vichare !!
So many other sing
they do not come to my mind
Says Nanak,
how can he consider them here.

!! Sayee Sayee Sadah Sach Sahib Saacha Saachi Nahi
That True Lord is True, Forever True
And True is His Name.
And His justice.

!! Hai Bhi Hosi Jae Na Jasi Rachnan Jini Rchaaii !!
He is and shall always be,
He shall not depart,
even when this Universe
which He has created departs.

!! Rangin Rangin Bhatii Kar Kar Jinsi Maya Jiji Upaaee !!
He created the world with its various colors,
species of beings and the variety of Maya.

!! Kar Kar Vekhai Kitaa Aapnann Jiv Tis di Vdiaaee !
Having created the creation,
He Himself watches over it
by His Greatness.

!! Jo Tis Bhaavhi Soee Karsi Hukam Na krnan Jaee !!
He does whatever He pleases.
No order can be issued to Him.

!! So Patsaahaa Pat Sahib Nanak rhin Rajaee !!
He is the king, the King of Kings.
The supreme Lord
Nanak remains subject to Him.

!! Step Twenty Eighth !!

(Yoga and its Way to Discipline Mind)

With contentment of mind as ear-rings,
Humility and service as bowl,
Meditation as ash to apply on the body,
Remembrance of death as the patched coat,
Purity of virginity as way of life,
Faith in Lord as the walking stick of self-confidence,
when a Yogi of this Temporal World steps out
to achieve something most precious of his life,
he becomes a winner of both the worlds.

!! Munda Santokh Sarm Patt Jholi Dhiaan ki Krhi Bibhuti !!
Make contentment our ear-rings,
Humility our begging bowl,
And meditation, the ashes we apply to our body.

!! Khintha Kaal Kuaari Kaaiaa Jugti Danda Prteet !!
Let the remembrance death be the patched coat we wear.
Let the purity of virginity be our way of life
in the world and let faith in the Lord be our walking stick.

!! Aaee Panthi Sagal Jmatee Man Jitai Jagjit !!
Honoring the brotherhood of mankind
as the highest order of yogis.
Winning our own mind is the victory of the world,
says Nanak, Let this one only be our religion
the 'Religion Divine'

!! Aades Tisai Aades !!
!! Aad Aneel Anaad Anaht Jug Jug Eko Ves !!
I bow Him. I humbly bow again and again
the Primal One. The Pure Light.
Without beginning. Without end.
Throughout all ages
He being one and the same.

!! Step Twenty Ninth !!

(Yoga and Its Way to Discipline Mind)

Let the store-keeper share his stores
Focusing his mind always on Divine Virtues,
Murmuring 'Tuun Hi Tuun' and 'Tera Hi Tera'.

Let the gardener of this world,
fix flowers of different colors, sizes and shapes
into one, the only one garland of whole of Humanity.

All these are the doable deeds.
All other Miraculous powers
are just blind bluffs and shots into darkness.

!! Bhugat Gian Daya Bhandarn Ghat Ghat Vaaje Naad !!
Let spiritual wisdom be our food.
Compassion our attendant.

Let Sound Current of Naad vibrate
in each and every heart.

Aap Naath Naathee Sabh Jaa Kee Ridhi Sidhi Avraa Saad !!
He Himself is the Supreme Master of all.
Wealth and miraculous powers,

and all other external tastes and pleasures
are different kinds of skills.

!! Sanjog Vijog Doae Kar Chlavhi Lekhai Aavhi Bhaag !!
Union with Him and separation from Him
comes by His Will.
We come to finally receive
what is written in our destiny
through Karma.

!! Aades Tisai Aades !!
!! Aad Aneel Anaad Anaht Jug Jug Eko Ves !!
I bow Him.
I humbly bow again and again
The Primal One. The Pure Light.
Without beginning. Without end.
Throughout all ages
He is one and the same.

!! Step Thirtieth !!

(Yoga and Its Way to Discipline Mind)

God is the Union of all the three,
The Creator, the Sustainer and Caretaker
of the house to see everything and everyone
in the house is in its proper order and at peace.

Doing this, He watches everything happening around
but nobody can see Him.
I praise His Egoless and Unconditional quality
of service for Humanity.

!! Ekaa Maaee Jugat Vaaee Tin Chele Parvaan !!
The One Divine Mother conceived
and gave birth to three Deities.

!! Ikk Sansari, Ikk Bhandari Ikk Laie Dibanu !!
One out of the three
First one is Creator of the Universe.
Second one is Sustainer
and third one is replenisher of the house.

!! Jiv Tis Bhaavai Tisai Chlavai Jiv Hovai Furmanu !!
He makes things Happen

according to the pleasure of His Will.
Such is the celestial order.

!! Oh Vekhaie Oh Nadar Na Aavhi Bhua Eho Vidaanu !!
He watches over all but no one see Him,
How wonderful this is !

!! Aades Tisai Aades !!
!! Aad Aneel Anaad Anaht Jug Jug Eko Ves !!
I bow Him. I humbly bow again and again,
the Primal One. The Pure Light.
Without beginning. Without end.
Throughout all ages
He is one and the same.

!! Step Thirty First !!

(Yoga and Its Way to Discipline Mind)

Not only in the three worlds,
His servants are working
at every place of this Universe.
Even in stones He serves food.
Even before we were born,
He first fixed food.
Yes, I salute His Kindness and Generosity.

!! Aasan Loay Loay Bhandar !!
On world after world are
His Seats of Authority and His Storehouses.

!! ji Kichhu Paaie So Eko Var !!
Whatever was put into the stores,
was put there once and for all.
Just in one blink of an eye.

!! Kar Kar Vekhai Sirjanhar !!
Having created the creation,
The creator Lord Watches over it.

!! Nanak Saache Kee Saachi Kaar !!
Says Nanak.
True is the creation of the True Lord.

!! Aades Tisai Aades !!
!! Aad Aneel Anaad Anaht Jug Jug Eko Ves !!

I bow Him.
I humbly bow again and again
The Primal One. The Pure Light.
Without beginning. Without end.
Throughout all ages
He is one and the same.

!! Step Thirty Second !!

(Our Beloved Kant and the Way to Reach Him)

Truth is the sum total of all the virtues.
That personify the soul of our beloved.

Climbing such steps of the ladder we finally reach Him.
Without using our brains and heart
and just coping others,
no one can reach His heights.
Cunningness, cleverness and bluffs
are just the signs of weakness.

!! Ikk Doo Jeebhao Lakh Hoiee Lakh Hoveh Lakh Vis !!
If I had hundred thousand tongues
And these are then multiplied by twenty times more,

!! Lakh Lakh Gedaa Akhiae Ek Nam Jagdish !!
When we repeat hundreds of thousands time that name
It becomes One, the name of The Lord.

!! Et Rahe Pat Pavdiaa Chadie Hoee Ikkis !!
Along this path to our Husband Lord,
we climb the steps of the ladder
and come to finally merge with Him.

!! Sun Galla Aakaas kita Aaee Rees !!
Hearing of His etheric realms,
even worms of the drain sometimes
long to come back home and be like Him.

!! Nanak Nadri Paaie Kudi Kude This !!
Says Nanak, by His Grace only he is obtained.
False are the boastings of the false.

!! Step Thirty Third !!

(Force Alone is not the Wisdom)

Wisdom is bigger, not the size of body or facial look.
Wisdom finally wins, may it be that of an ant.

Something good done for self and society by use of brain
is much better than many things done by use of force.

Yes, we can take an unbridled horse
of our mind to the pond by force
but cannot make him drink against his will.

History is witness to the fact,
World wars applying use of force killed
Hundreds of thousands innocent lives
With an unimaginable damages of property.

!! Aakhn Jor Chupai Na Jor !!
No power can force us to speak
if we don't want to speak.

No power can keep us silent
if we don't want to keep silent.

!! Jor Na Mangan Dein Na Jor !!
No power can make us beg
if we don't want to beg.

No power can make us give
if we don't want to give.

!! Jor Na Jivan Marn Na Jor !!
No power can make us live
if we don't want to live.

No power can make us die
if don't want to die.

!! Jor Na Raj Maal Man Soru !!
No power can rule over others
with wealth and occult mental powers.

!! Jor Na Surti Giaan Vichaar !!
No power can gain intuitive understanding,
spiritual wisdom and meditation without
His Blessings.

!! Jor Na Jugati Chhutai Sansar !!
No power can find the way
to escape safe from the world.
Guru Gobind Singh ji found the way out
in the darkness only with His Blessings.

!! Jis Hath Jor Kar Vaykhai Soe !!
He alone has the Power in His hands.
And He watches over us.

!! Nanak Uttam Neech Na Koe !!

Not necessary and no guarantee
Says Nanak,
that by the use of power alone
someone can be High or Low,

!! Step Thirty Fourth !!

(Final Judgement Based on the Deeds Done)

In the vast expanse of nature,
It finally is the noble and good deeds
based on which sane and sinners
are finally separated for a place to
Heaven or Hell.

!! Rati Ruti Thitti Vaar !!
Nights, days, weeks, months,
and seasons of the year.

!! Pavan Pani Agnin Pataal !!
Wind, water, fire
and nether regions

!! Tis Wich Dhart Thaap Rakhi Dharmsal !!
In the midst of these,
He established Earth
as a home to do Dharma.

!! Tis Wich Jia Jugat ke Rang !!
Upon it, He placed
various species of beings.

!! Tin ke Nam Anek Anant !!
Their names are
Countless and Endless.

!! Karmin Karmin Hoie Vichar !!
By their deeds and their actions only
they shall be judged.

!! Saacha Aap Saacha Darbar !!
God Himself is true
and true is His Court.

!! Tithay Sohan Panch Parvanu !!
There, in perfect grace and ease
sit the self-elects, the self-realized Saints.

!! Nadri Karmin pave Neesan !!
They receive the Mark of Grace
from the Merciful Lord.

!! Kach Pkaaee Othe Paaie !!
The ripe and unripe,
the good and bad,
Shall there be judged.

!! Nanak Giaa Jaapai jaa-ay !!
Says Nanak, when we go home,
we will see it and realize it.

!! Step Thirty Fifth !!

(Realms of Religion and Knowledge)

Everything illustrated above
pertains to Realm of Dharma, the Religion.
This realm talks about so many things
like Water, fire and so many different worlds.

So many saints, seers, teachers, preachers,
intellectuals, philosophers and others.

!! Dharmu Khand Ka Eho Dharm !!
!! Gian Khand Ka Aakhhu Karam !!.
Illustrated and explained above
Is the Realm of Dharmu Khand
And now we speak about
The Realm of Spiritual Wisdom.

!! Kete Pavan Paani Baisantar Kete Kahn Mahesh !!
There are So many kinds of winds, waters and fires
and so many Sages and Sears like Krishna and Shiva,
the oratory of the Spirit of the word Truth.

!! Kete Barmay Ghadat Ghdie Roop Rang Ke Ves !!
So many Brahmas fashning forms of great beauty
adorned and dressed in many colors.

!! Ketia Karan Bhumin Mer Kete Kete Dhuu Updedh !!
So many worlds and lands for working out Karma.
So many lessons to be learnt from bhagats like Dhruva.

!! kete Ind Chand Suur Kete Kete Mandal Des !!
So many are Indras.
So many are Suns and Moons.
So many are worlds and lands.

!! Kete Sidh Budh Nath Kete Kete Devi Ves !!
There are so many Sidhas and Budhas.
So many are Yogic Masers.
So many goddesses of various kinds.

!! Kete Dev Danav Mun Lete Kete Ratan Samund !!
So many are demi-gods and demons.
There are so many silent sages.
There are so many oceans of jewels.

!! Keta Khani Ketia Bani Kete Pat Nrind !!
There are so many ways of life.
So many languages
and so many dynasties of rulers.

!! Ketia Surti Sevak Kete Nanak Ant Na Ant !!
There are so many intuitive people.
So many selfless servants.
Says Nanak,
There is no limit.

!! Step Thirty Six !!

(Realms of Knowledge and Humility)

This Realm of knowledge,
The knowledge of Universe,
its Creator and its Creation takes the
'Spirit of our Self Confidence'
To the level like that of Chandi,
the Kalka Devi,
The Goddess of Strength.
Nar Singh, the killer of Kans.

All kinds of fears in this Realm,
including the fear of death vanish.

<u>Gian Khans Meh Gian Parchand !!</u>
The second realm is the Realm of
Spiritual Knowledge of Truth, the Gian Khand.
In the realm of wisdom spiritual wisdom reigns supreme.

!! Tithe Naad Vinod Kod Aanad !!
The sound current of Naad vibrates there
amidst the sound and sites of bliss.

!! Saram Khand Ki Bani Roop !!
The word of this third
Realm of Saram Khand,
The Realm of Beauty is Humility.
Down to the Earth Humility.

!! Tithe Ghadat Ghadie Bhut Anup !!
Forms of incomparable beauty
are fashioned there.

!! Ta Kia Gllan Kthiaa Na Jae !!
These things cannot be described
through any vocabulary of words.

!! Je Ko Khe Pichhe Pachhutai !!
One who tries to speak of these,
shall regret the attempt.

!! Tithe Ghadie Surat Mat Man Budh !!
In intuitive consciousness,
intellect and understanding of mind
are shaped there.

!! Tithe Ghadie Sura Sidha Ki Sudh !!
Like Banda Singh Bhadur,
In the consciousness of spiritual warriors and Sidhas,
the beings of spiritual perfection are shaped there.

!! Step Thirty Seventh !!

(Realms of Power and Truth)

This Realm is the Realm of Power, the Will Power.
the power of extreme self-esteem and confidence
generated by blessings of Lord.

In this Realm dwell,
the Saints and Soldiers like Guru Gobind Singh Ji
and Sadhus, like Rama, Yudhishtra, the sach-putra,
whose minds always stayed focused and fixed in Lord.

!! Karam Khand Ki Bani Jor !!
The word of this third khand, is Jor,
the Power, the realm of Karma, The Action,
which originates from Practice of Holy word.

!! Tithe Hor Na koi Hor !!
No one else dwells there
other than only Him the All Powerful.

!! Tithai Jodh Mhanbal Suur !!
Except the warriors of great power, t
he spiritual heroes, there is no one else.

!! Tin Mhi Ram Rhiaa Bharpur !!
They are totally fulfilled,
imbued with the Lord's Essence.

!! Tithe Sito Sita Mhima Mahi !!
Myriads of Sitas are there,
cool and calm in their majestic glory.

!! Ta Ka Roop Na Kathna Jaae !!
Their beauty cannot be described
But Yes, that beauty can be enjoyed by meditating,
practicing and inhibiting their virtues.

!! Na oh Mre Na Thaage Jaaie !!
Neither death, nor deception comes close
to such blessed and God approved Believers.

!! Jin Ke Ram Vsai Man Mahie !!
Such blessed Souls maintain peace for all the times.
Ghosts of Anger stay always away from such servant of God.

!! Tithae Bhagat Ke Loaa !!
The devotees of many worlds dwell there.
If there are bad people
Here in our world,
there are countless good people
in His World
for us therefore,
It simply is a question
of making better choices.

!! Karhi Anand Sacha Man Soay !!
They always celebrate
and their minds are imbued
with the spirit of True Lord.

!! Sach Khand Vsai Nirnkar !!
In the Realm of Truth,
The Formless Lord resides.
Only the 'Peace' resides.

!! Kar Kar Vekhai Nadri Nihaal !!
Having created the creation,
he watches over it.
By His Glance of Grace
He bestows happiness.

!! Tithai Khand Mandal Varbhand !!
There are planets,
solar systems and Galaxies.

!! Je ko Kathe Ta Ant Na Ant !!
If one speaks of them,
there is no count and no end.
See, how mystical this thought is!

!! Tithai Loaa Loaa Aakar !!
There are worlds upon worlds
of His creation.

!! Jiv Jiv Hukam Tivai Tiv Kaar !!
As He Commands,
So we exist.

!! Vekhai Vigsai Kar Vichaar !!
He watches over all.
Contemplating the creation.
He rejoices doing so.

!! Nanak Kthnan Karda Saar !!
It is easy to say
Says Nanak, But not so easy
to Live, Love and Practice the Truth.

!! Step Thirty Eight Eight !!

(Minting of Mind like the Mint by Goldsmith)

Like the mint of a goldsmith,
wherein the cool minded goldsmith,
mints countless pieces of beautiful
and costly jewelry after refining the gold in fires.

In this Realm of Truth same way,
He, the Lord mints countless gems and Jewels

!! Jat Pahara Dhiraj Suniaar !!
Let self-control be the furnace
and patient the goldsmith

!! Ahiran Matt Ved Hthiaar !!
Let understanding be the anvil
and spiritual wisdom the hammer.

!! Bhao Khlaa Agan Tap Taoo !!
With Fear of God as the bellows,
fan the flames of Tapa,
the body's inner heat.

!! Bhanda Bhao Amrit Tit Dhaal !!
In the crucible of love,
melt da Nectar of the Name

!! Ghadie Shabad Sachi Taksal !!
Mint the true coin of Shabad,
The Word of God.

!! Jin Kao Nadri Karm Tin Kaar !!
Such is the destiny (Karma)
of those upon whom He has cast
His Glance of Grace.

!! Nanak Nadri Nadar Nihal !!
Only such Believers achieve
"Everlasting Bliss and Eternal Life"
Says Nanak,
The Merciful Lord by His Grace,
uplifts and exhalts them.

!! Closing Slok of Japuji Sahib Ji !!

!! Pavan Guru Pani Pita Mata Dhart Mhat !!
Air is the Guru, the source of
'Spiritual Knowledge'
Water is the Father,
and the Earth the Great Mother of all.

!! Divas Raat Doe Daaee Daaia Khelai Sgal Jgat !!
Day and night are the two nurses,
in whose lap all the world is at play.

!! Changiaeean Buriaian vachai Dharam Hadoor !!
Good deeds and bad deeds record
is read out in the Presence of the lord of Dharma.

!! Karmin Aapo Aapnin Kay Nerhe Ke Door !!
According to our own actions,
some are drawn closer
while some others are driven farther away.

!! Jinin Nam Dhiaie Gae Msakt Ghaal !!
Those who have meditated on Him,

Those who have worked hard
in practicing the Truth, His Word,
are blessed by Him.

!! Nanak Te Mukh Ujjle Kete Chhutti Nal !!
Their faces are radiant in the 'Court of the Lord'
And many others are saved along with them.

PART FOUR
General

Realms of Achieving Him

Five Realms of Reaching the Land of Truth
Five Realms of reaching Our Beloved
Sitting at the core of our heart are:-

Realm of Religion
This Realm of Religion fully equips the man
of this temporal world
with all the virtues like Truth,
Love, Kindness, Compassion and Forgiveness
to deal with both the worlds,
Material and Spiritual,
exactly the way a good student
gets himself fully equipped in the school.

Realm of Knowledge
The knowledge of Universe,
its Creator and its Creation
takes the 'Spirit of our Self Confidence'
To the level like that of Chandi,
the Kalka Devi, The Goddess of Strength.

All kinds of fears in this Realm,
including the fear of death vanish.

Realm of Humility

This Realm of Humility
adds the essence of natural beauty
to the heights of Mira,
the worshiper of Lord Krishnan.

Fully immersed in the virtues of Humility
Purity of mind and service to humanity,
This Realm earns the respect and blessings
for such humble servants from both the worlds.

Realm of Power

Attaining knowledge and humility,
after realm of Religion, the Dharm Khand,
this Realm further adds the element of Power
to make humans attain the attributes of a Creator.

In this Realm even a single man
at the age of a child develops the courage
and strength to face and fight with
hundreds of thousands in the war field.

Even the man shivering and shaking his hands
with fear and duality of mind,
develops the courage and strength
to fight in the war field.

Realm of Truth

This is the realm of Saints and soldiers
Wherein words like me, mine and thine
merge into melody of 'One'
The Super-Natural 'One'

where Saints and soldiers
share stores of Divine virtues
murmuring Holy Words
like 'Tuun Hi Tuun'
and 'Tera Hi Tera'.

Where humblest of the humble Sudaman
The Cloth-Sticher Namdev,
The Shoe-Maker Ravidas
The farmer Dhanna
The cloth craftsman Kabir
on the sheer strength of their humbleness
and truthfulness make even their Masters
listen and obey their command to serve them.

About the Author

Born in a farmer's family of India, Mr. Amrik Binapal worked as a Mechanical Engineer in a big Public sector undertaking of India for about thirty-one years.

He lost his wife at her young age of Forty-five in March 1991.

He has two grown up children, both of whom are presently working as physicians in the state of Georgia USA.

At the age of about seventy-nine, he is now retired and taking care of his grandchildren.

By now he has written four books in English which are: Quest for Peace, Absolute Truth, Religion Divine and A Glimpse At My Mind.

He has also written two books in his native language Punjabi which are:
Sach Jiven Mainu Laggia and Sangit Atman Da.

Contact information:
Vill.Isru, Distt.Ludhiana (Pb) India.
E-Mail amrik350@yahoo.com
Ph # 001-706-936-1015 (USA)

About the Book

The book under the title 'Holy Word of Japuji Sahib Ji'
details and explains the 'Attributes' of the most
Beautiful and Powerful God Head we all seek
to be the captain of the ship of our lives.

The book also explains that meditating and practicing
the spirit of these attributes every day in life,
the seeker one day will surely be with Him
and be like Him.

After the word of meditation, the book further details
thirty-eight steps of the wisdom and the way to truth
and the life.

It merely is not the reading, teaching and preaching
of the Holy Word the book explains, it is the sincere
practice of 'The Spirit of Holy Word' which is the key
to finally open us the doors of 'Kingdom of God'

He, 'The Spirit of Truth and Love' cannot be
expressed in words but yes
He can be very well realized, lived and enjoyed
by meditating and practicing the Truth.

CPSIA information can be obtained
at www.ICGtesting.com
Printed in the USA
BVHW031406300620
582558BV00017B/104